WHITE HOUSE INSIDERS

What's It Like to Be the
PRESIDENT?

BY KATHLEEN CONNORS

 Gareth Stevens
PUBLISHING

Please visit our website, www.garethstevens.com. For a free color catalog of all our high-quality books, call toll free 1-800-542-2595 or fax 1-877-542-2596.

Library of Congress Cataloging-in-Publication Data

Connors, Kathleen.
What's it like to be the President? / by Kathleen Connors.
  p. cm. — (White House insiders)
Includes index.
ISBN 978-1-4824-1096-9 (pbk.)
ISBN 978-1-4824-1097-6 (6-pack)
ISBN 978-1-4824-1095-2 (library binding)
1. Presidents — United States — Juvenile literature. I. Connors, Kathleen. II. Title.
JK517.C66 2014
353.03—d23

First Edition

Published in 2015 by
Gareth Stevens Publishing
111 East 14th Street, Suite 349
New York, NY 10003

Designer: Nick Domiano
Editor: Kristen Rajczak

Photo credits: Cover, p. 1 (Barack Obama) Olivier Douliery-Pool/Getty Images News/Getty Images; cover, p. 1 (George H. Bush) Renaud Giroux/AFP/Getty Images; cover, p. 1 (Bill Clinton) Richard Ellis/Hulton Archive/Getty Images; p. 5 Emmanuel Dunand/AFP/Getty Images; p. 7 Hulton Archive/Getty Images; p. 9 Eric Draper/Getty Images News/Getty Images; p. 11 Chip Somodevilla/Getty Images News/Getty images; p. 13 Moshe Miller/Hulton Archive/Getty Images; p. 15 Universal Images Group/Getty Images; p. 17 Timur Emek/Getty Images News/Getty Images; p. 17 (inset) Time & Life Pictures/White House/Getty Images; p. 19 Tim Sloan/AFP/Getty Images; p. 20 (inset) Arne Knudsen/Getty Images News/Getty Images.

Printed in the United States of America

CPSIA compliance information: Batch #CS15GS: For further information contact Gareth Stevens, New York, New York at 1-800-542-2595.

Contents

Words in the glossary appear in **bold** type the first time they are used in the text.

POTUS

President is the highest **political** office in the United States. Some people call the president the "leader of the free world." Other names are POTUS, a shortening of **p**resident **o**f **t**he **U**nited **S**tates, or Mr. President. If a woman becomes president, she'll be called Madame President.

The presidency has changed a lot since George Washington took office in 1789. Today, the president is always in the public eye and juggling many issues at once. How does he do it—and still have time to eat dinner?

The Inside Scoop

As the first US president, George Washington set many **precedents**. However, he didn't really want the position. Some historians say he became president partly because he needed a job!

President Barack Obama has said he tries to be home for dinner as often as possible. He likes to talk to his daughters and wife about their day and take a break from his!

5

Presidential Duties

According to the US **Constitution**, the president must be at least 35 years old, have been born in the United States, and have lived in the United States for at least 14 years. The president's main job is to **enforce** the laws of the nation and keep the central government running. The Constitution also makes the president the commander in chief of the military.

These are weighty tasks for one person! That's why the Constitution also gives the president powers to appoint top officials like judges and **ambassadors**.

The Inside Scoop

The president's closest advisers are members of the Cabinet. But the Senate must approve Cabinet appointees. President Andrew Jackson wanted more power over his advisers than that, so he also assembled an unofficial group called the "Kitchen Cabinet."

The president appoints many governmental positions. At left, President Franklin D. Roosevelt looks on as a new secretary of the navy is sworn in by Supreme Court Justice Felix Frankfurter, right.

A Day in the Life

On April 28, 1975, President Gerald Ford's daily diary reveals he woke up at 6:50 a.m. and was in the Oval Office by around 7:30 a.m. He spoke with top advisers, went to a meeting of the National Security Council, and met with several groups until 9:15 p.m., when he had dinner with the First Lady. After that, he continued working until around midnight.

This one example, gathered from the Gerald R. Ford Presidential Library and Museum, shows the nonstop days of modern presidents.

The Inside Scoop

George Washington was paid $25,000 a year to be president, which equals about $1 million today! President Bill Clinton raised the president's salary to $400,000 a year, which came into effect in 2001 after his presidency.

Modern presidents have to speak to the press often and are given little privacy. After his presidency ended in 2009, President George W. Bush (left) said, "There's really no sacrifice in serving the country...but if there is one, it's loss of **anonymity**."

9

Home Sweet Home

One of the major perks of being president is living in the White House. The president and the president's family live in the East Wing of the White House, while the president's offices are in the West Wing. That means the president can just walk to work!

The White House has a full-time staff including professional chefs and a doctor. There's a movie theater and bowling alley! The White House even has a tennis court, which President Barack Obama has also used for basketball.

The Inside Scoop

Presidents and their families often make changes to the White House when they move in. Many redecorate. Lyndon Johnson installed TVs and phones in each of his bathrooms so he could always be reached.

In 2011, President Barack Obama invited players from the Harlem Globetrotters to shoot some hoops on the basketball court he had remodeled at the White House.

11

What Days Off?

President Franklin D. Roosevelt led the United States during the **Great Depression** and into World War II. But even great leaders need a break! In 1942, Roosevelt established the presidential retreat in Maryland that's called Camp David today. The use of this lovely country home is one of the big perks of being president!

Though Camp David is used for presidents' rare days off, the president isn't ever completely away from work. Sometimes foreign leaders are brought there for work, too.

The Inside Scoop

Another perk of living at the White House is getting married there! President Richard Nixon's daughter Tricia married her husband in the White House Rose Garden in 1971.

In 1978, the Israeli prime minister (right) met with President Jimmy Carter (center) and the president of Egypt (left) at Camp David to discuss peace between the two nations.

Head of the Household

Even though he's called Mr. President at work, many presidents go by another name—Dad! In fact, only six presidents didn't have children.

George H. W. Bush had six grown children when he became president in 1989. One of them, George W. Bush, became president just 8 years after his father left office! They were the second father and son pair to be president. John Adams was president from 1797 to 1801, and his son John Quincy Adams served from 1825 to 1829.

The Inside Scoop

The White House South Lawn was like a playground when President Kennedy was in office! His two small children had a swing set and jungle gym there. Malia and Sasha Obama have also had a swing set on the White House lawn.

President John Tyler had 15 children!
He was married twice.

15

Abroad on Air Force One

George Washington wanted the United States to stay out of other nations' troubles. However, modern presidents travel around the world to meet with foreign leaders about trade, conflicts, and other issues. The president has become the face of the United States to the world.

The president often uses Air Force One when he needs to fly. Air Force One is any US Air Force jet the president is in, but the name is more commonly used for the two Boeing 747s made for presidential travel.

The Inside Scoop

Air Force One has three levels and includes an office for the president; a meeting room; beds for the president, his staff, and advisers; and two kitchens!

Bill Clinton

Air Force One is a safe place for the president. It can be refueled while in the air so it can keep flying to wherever the president needs to go—or if the president needs to stay in the air.

Personal Appeal

The president hasn't just been all over the world—he's been all over the nation! Sometimes, he's giving speeches, as President Obama did at Morehouse College in May 2013. He may meet with groups that want certain **legislation** passed or to learn more about concerns of regular Americans.

President Bill Clinton visited Columbine, Colorado, in 1999 after a terrible shooting occurred. The president's presence at scenes of natural **disaster** and **tragedy** like the Columbine shooting gives people hope. It helps show the government cares.

The Inside Scoop

All presidents have speechwriters. How much the president writes often depends on the occasion and the topic. The president might be less concerned about a short welcome speech at an informal dinner and more interested in the **State of the Union**.

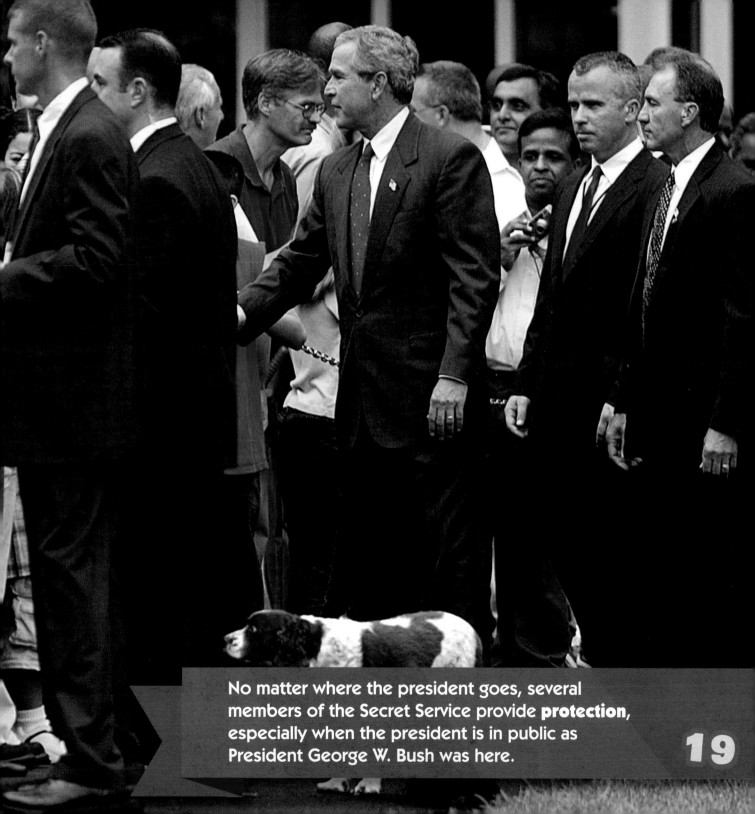

No matter where the president goes, several members of the Secret Service provide **protection**, especially when the president is in public as President George W. Bush was here.

19

After Office

After President Franklin D. Roosevelt was elected to four terms as president, it became law that no president could serve more than two terms. That's not a very long time!

Former presidents now receive almost $200,000 a year, an office, a staff, and money for travel paid for by the US government. They often continue to fight for legislation and issues they care about. Jimmy Carter received the Nobel Peace Prize in 2002 for his ongoing peace work in countries around the world!

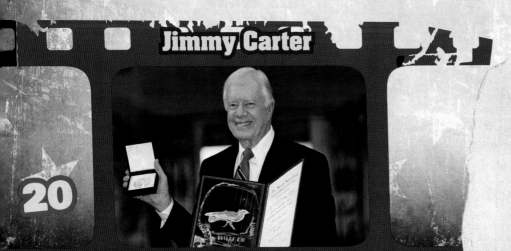

Jimmy Carter

20

The Inside Scoop

If the president dies while in office, the vice president becomes president. This has happened eight times.

Presidential Favorites

Foods

- Gerald Ford loved a dinner of pot roast, red cabbage, and butter pecan ice cream.

- Jimmy Carter enjoyed cornbread.

Sports

- Dwight Eisenhower spent a lot of time playing golf.

- George W. Bush loved baseball so much he was once an owner of the Texas Rangers baseball team.

Music

- Thomas Jefferson played violin. He liked to sing Scottish and Italian songs, too.

- Bill Clinton played the saxophone and listened to the band Fleetwood Mac.

Glossary

ambassador: someone sent by one group or country to speak for it in different places

anonymity: the state of being unrecognized, especially by the general public

constitution: the basic laws by which a country or state is governed

disaster: an event that causes much suffering or loss

enforce: to make sure people obey the law

Great Depression: a period of economic troubles with widespread unemployment and poverty (1929–1939)

legislation: laws

political: having to do with the activities of the government and government officials

precedent: something done or said in the past that sets a model for the future

protection: the act of keeping safe

State of the Union: the yearly speech the president gives to Congress about the state of the country

tragedy: a terrible event

For More Information

BOOKS

Barber, James. *Presidents*. New York, NY: Dorling Kindersley, 2009.

Jennings, Ken. *U.S. Presidents*. New York, NY: Little Simon, 2014.

WEBSITES

President for a Day
pbskids.org/democracy/be-president/
See what it's like to be president in this online activity. Also, learn more about the presidency.

The Presidents
www.whitehouse.gov/about/presidents
Learn about each president's life on the White House website.

Index